# Guess What

Published in the United States of America by
**Cherry Lake Publishing**
Ann Arbor, Michigan
www.cherrylakepublishing.com

Content Adviser: Susan Heinrichs Gray
Reading Adviser: Marla Conn, ReadAbility, Inc.
Book Designer: Felicia Macheske

Photo Credits: © dive-hive/Shutterstock Images, cover, 7; © Hans Gert Broeder/Shutterstock Images, 1, 4; © Rich Carey/ Shutterstock Images, 3, 9, 11; © frantisekhojdysz/Shutterstock Images, 13; © JHVEPhoto/Shutterstock Images, 14; © David Evison/Shutterstock Images, 17; photostock77/Shutterstock Images, 18; © serg_dibrova/Shutterstock Images, 21; © Andrey_ Kuzmin/Shutterstock Images, back cover; © Eric Isselee/Shutterstock Images, back cover

Library of Congress Cataloging-in-Publication Data

Macheske, Felicia, author.
 Flying flippers : sea turtle / Macheske, Felicia.
 pages cm. — (Guess what)
 Summary: "Young children are natural problem solvers and always looking for answers, especially when it involves ocean animals. Guess What: Flying Flippers: Sea Turtle provides young curious readers with striking visual clues and simply written hints. Using the photos and text, readers rely on visual literacy skills, reading, and reasoning as they solve the animal mystery. Clearly written facts give readers a deeper understanding of how the sea turtle lives. Additional text features, including a glossary and an index, help students locate information and learn new words"— Provided by publisher.
 Audience: K to grade 3.
 Includes index.
 ISBN 978-1-63470-716-9 (hardcover) — ISBN 978-1-63470-746-6 (pbk.) — ISBN 978-1-63470-731-2 (pdf) — ISBN 978-1-63470-761-9 (ebook)
 1. Sea turtles—Juvenile literature. 2. Children's questions and answers. I. Title.
 QL666.C536M332 2016
 597.92'8—dc23
 2015026086

Cherry Lake Publishing would like to acknowledge the work of The Partnership for 21st Century Skills.
Please visit *www.p21.org* for more information.

Printed in the United States of America
Corporate Graphics

# Table of Contents

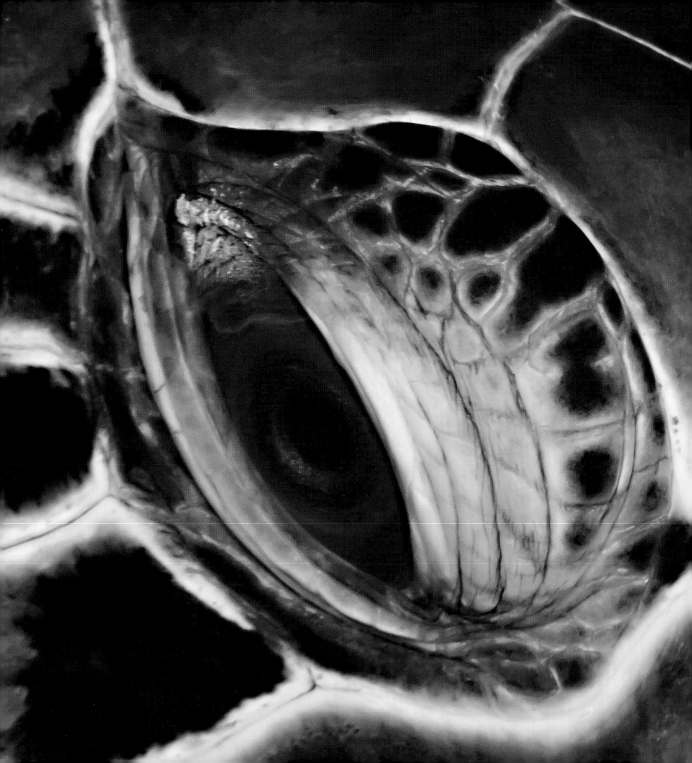

I can
see well
when I am
underwater.

# I have flippers that help me swim.

I don't have any teeth in my mouth.

# I have a shell that protects my body.

# I spend most of my time in the ocean.

# But I still need to come up for air.

# I hatched from an egg laid in the sand.

# Then I had to **run** to the ocean.

**Do you know what I am?**

# I'm a Sea Turtle!

# About Sea Turtles

1. There are seven **species** of sea turtles.

2. Unlike many land turtles, sea turtles cannot tuck their heads inside their shells.

3. Sea turtles are very good swimmers. Their flippers are like paddles in the water.

4. Many sea turtles **migrate** a long way to find food and to **breed**.

5. Sea turtles lay their eggs on land. Then they leave the eggs behind.

# Glossary

**breed** (BREED) to join together and have babies

**flippers** (FLIP-urz) broad, flat body parts that sea animals use for swimming

**hatched** (HACHD) broke out of an egg

**migrate** (MYE-grate) to move from one area to another

**species** (SPEE-sheez) one of the groups into which animals and plants are divided

# Index